ROLAND PARKER

Mastering Python Interviews
Essential Coding Problems and Solutions for Success

Copyright © 2024 by Roland Parker

All rights reserved. No part of this publication may be reproduced, stored or transmitted in any form or by any means, electronic, mechanical, photocopying, recording, scanning, or otherwise without written permission from the publisher. It is illegal to copy this book, post it to a website, or distribute it by any other means without permission.

First edition

This book was professionally typeset on Reedsy. Find out more at reedsy.com

Contents

Introduction	1
The Interview Process	5
Python Basics	11
Data Structures	29
Algorithms	40
Advanced Topics	47
Coding Problems	53
System Design	61
Behavioral Questions	66
Mock Interviews	71
Appendices	76

Introduction

Welcome to the World of Programming Interviews

Welcome to the world of programming interviews, a realm where your coding skills, problem-solving abilities, and technical knowledge are put to the test. Whether you're a seasoned developer or a recent graduate, preparing for programming interviews can be a daunting task. This book is designed to be your comprehensive guide, helping you navigate the complexities of technical interviews and emerge victorious.

Programming interviews are a critical step in the hiring process for many tech companies. They are designed to assess your ability to think logically, solve problems efficiently, and write clean, maintainable code. These interviews often include a mix of algorithmic challenges, data structure problems, and system design questions. The goal is to evaluate not only your technical skills but also your ability to communicate your thought process and work collaboratively.

In this book, we will focus on Python, a versatile and powerful programming language that is widely used in the tech industry. Python's simplicity and readability make it an excellent choice for coding interviews, allowing you to focus on solving the problem rather than getting bogged down by complex syntax. By mastering the elements of programming interviews in Python, you will be well-equipped to tackle any challenge that comes your way.

How to Use This Book

This book is structured to provide you with a step-by-step guide to mastering programming interviews. Each chapter is designed to build on the previous one, gradually increasing in complexity and covering a wide range of topics. Here's how you can make the most of this book:

1. Start with the Basics: If you're new to Python or need a refresher, begin with the chapters on Python basics. These chapters will cover the fundamental concepts and syntax of Python, ensuring you have a solid foundation before diving into more complex topics.
2. Focus on Data Structures and Algorithms: The core of any programming interview is your understanding of data structures and algorithms. Spend ample time on these chapters, practicing the problems and understanding the underlying concepts. This will be crucial for solving the majority of interview questions.
3. Practice Coding Problems: The book includes a wide range of coding problems, categorized by topic. Practice these problems regularly, and try to solve them without looking at the solutions. This will help you develop your problem-solving skills and build confidence.
4. Review System Design: For senior-level positions, system design questions are common. The chapters on system design will provide you with the knowledge and tools to tackle these questions effectively. Pay attention to the case studies and examples, as they will give you insights into real-world scenarios.
5. Prepare for Behavioral Questions: Technical skills are important, but so are your soft skills. The chapter on behavioral questions will help you prepare for this aspect of the interview. Practice answering common questions using the STAR method (Situation, Task, Action, Result) to structure your responses.
6. Conduct Mock Interviews: Use the mock interview section to simulate real interview scenarios. This will help you get comfortable with the interview format and improve your performance under pressure. Analyze your performance and identify areas for improvement.
7. Utilize the Appendices: The appendices contain valuable resources, including a Python standard library reference, common algorithms and data structures, and an interview preparation checklist. Refer to these

INTRODUCTION

resources as needed to reinforce your learning.

By following this structured approach, you will be well-prepared for your programming interviews. Remember, practice and persistence are key. The more you practice, the more confident and proficient you will become.

Overview of Python for Interviews

Python is a high-level, interpreted programming language known for its simplicity and readability. It has become one of the most popular languages in the tech industry, used by companies like Google, Facebook, and Amazon. Python's versatility makes it suitable for a wide range of applications, from web development to data science and machine learning.

For programming interviews, Python offers several advantages:

1. Readability: Python's clean and straightforward syntax allows you to write code that is easy to read and understand. This is particularly important in interviews, where you need to communicate your thought process clearly to the interviewer.
2. Rich Standard Library: Python comes with a comprehensive standard library that provides modules and functions for various tasks, such as file handling, data manipulation, and networking. This can save you time and effort during the interview.
3. Dynamic Typing: Python's dynamic typing system allows you to write code quickly without worrying about explicit type declarations. This can be a significant advantage in time-constrained interview scenarios.
4. Extensive Community Support: Python has a large and active community of developers who contribute to a wealth of resources, including libraries, frameworks, and tutorials. This means you have access to a vast amount of knowledge and tools to aid your preparation.

In this book, we will leverage Python's strengths to solve a variety of interview problems. You will learn how to implement common data structures and algorithms in Python, write efficient and optimized code, and tackle complex coding challenges. By the end of this book, you will have a deep understanding of Python and be well-prepared to ace your programming interviews.

Welcome to the journey of mastering programming interviews in Python. Let's get started!

The Interview Process

Preparing for the Interview

Preparation is the cornerstone of success in any programming interview. The more thoroughly you prepare, the more confident and capable you will feel during the actual interview. Here are some key steps to ensure you are well-prepared:

1. **Understand the Job Requirements**: Start by thoroughly reading the job description and understanding the skills and qualifications required. Identify the key areas where you need to focus your preparation. This will help you tailor your study plan to the specific needs of the role.
2. **Research the Company**: Learn about the company's products, services, culture, and recent news. This knowledge will not only help you answer questions about why you want to work there but also enable you to ask insightful questions during the interview. Understanding the company's tech stack and the problems they are solving can give you a competitive edge.
3. **Review Core Concepts**: Brush up on fundamental concepts in computer science, such as data structures, algorithms, and system design. Make sure you understand the basics of Python, including syntax, data types, control structures, and common libraries. Use resources like textbooks, online courses, and coding platforms to reinforce your knowledge.
4. **Practice Coding Problems**: Regular practice is essential for mastering coding problems. Use platforms like LeetCode, HackerRank, and CodeS-

ignal to solve a variety of problems. Focus on different categories, such as arrays, strings, linked lists, trees, graphs, and dynamic programming. Time yourself to simulate real interview conditions and improve your speed and accuracy.

5. **Mock Interviews**: Conduct mock interviews with friends, mentors, or through online services. Mock interviews help you get comfortable with the interview format and receive constructive feedback. Analyze your performance, identify areas for improvement, and work on them.
6. **Prepare Behavioral Answers**: Behavioral questions are a significant part of the interview process. Use the STAR method (Situation, Task, Action, Result) to structure your answers. Prepare examples that highlight your problem-solving skills, teamwork, leadership, and adaptability. Practice articulating your experiences clearly and concisely.
7. **Review System Design**: For senior-level positions, system design questions are common. Study the principles of designing scalable and efficient systems. Understand concepts like load balancing, caching, database design, and microservices. Practice designing systems for common scenarios, such as social media platforms, e-commerce websites, and messaging apps.
8. **Prepare Your Questions**: Interviews are a two-way street. Prepare thoughtful questions to ask the interviewer about the role, team, company culture, and future projects. This shows your genuine interest in the position and helps you assess if the company is the right fit for you.

Common Interview Mistakes

Even with thorough preparation, candidates can make mistakes during interviews. Being aware of these common pitfalls can help you avoid them:

1. **Lack of Preparation**: Underestimating the importance of preparation is a common mistake. Failing to review core concepts, practice coding problems, or research the company can leave you unprepared and anxious during the interview.

2. **Poor Communication**: Effective communication is crucial in interviews. Avoid being too brief or too verbose in your answers. Clearly explain your thought process, reasoning, and approach to solving problems. If you get stuck, communicate your challenges and ask for clarification if needed.
3. **Ignoring Edge Cases**: When solving coding problems, it's essential to consider edge cases and test your solution thoroughly. Ignoring edge cases can lead to incomplete or incorrect solutions. Always think about potential inputs that could break your code and handle them appropriately.
4. **Overcomplicating Solutions**: Sometimes candidates try to impress interviewers with overly complex solutions. Focus on writing clean, simple, and efficient code. If you have time, you can discuss potential optimizations, but start with a straightforward approach.
5. **Lack of Confidence**: Confidence plays a significant role in interviews. Doubting your abilities or second-guessing your answers can negatively impact your performance. Trust in your preparation and skills, and approach each question with a positive mindset.
6. **Not Asking Questions**: Failing to ask questions at the end of the interview can be seen as a lack of interest. Prepare a list of thoughtful questions to ask the interviewer. This demonstrates your enthusiasm for the role and helps you gather valuable information.
7. **Neglecting Behavioral Questions**: Focusing solely on technical preparation and neglecting behavioral questions is a common mistake. Behavioral questions assess your soft skills and cultural fit. Prepare and practice answers to common behavioral questions to present yourself as a well-rounded candidate.

Strategies for a Successful Interview

To maximize your chances of success, adopt the following strategies during your interview:

1. **Stay Calm and Focused**: Interviews can be stressful, but staying calm

and focused is essential. Take deep breaths, listen carefully to the questions, and take your time to think before answering. If you don't know the answer immediately, it's okay to ask for a moment to gather your thoughts.
2. **Break Down Problems**: When faced with a coding problem, break it down into smaller, manageable parts. Explain your approach step-by-step and write pseudocode if necessary. This helps you organize your thoughts and makes it easier for the interviewer to follow your logic.
3. **Think Aloud**: Verbalize your thought process as you work through problems. This allows the interviewer to understand your reasoning and provides insight into your problem-solving skills. It also helps you stay focused and avoid getting stuck.
4. **Test Your Code**: After writing your solution, test it with different inputs, including edge cases. Walk through your code line by line to ensure it works as expected. This demonstrates your attention to detail and thoroughness.
5. **Be Honest**: If you don't know the answer to a question, be honest about it. It's better to admit your limitations than to provide incorrect information. You can discuss how you would approach finding the answer or ask for guidance.
6. **Show Enthusiasm**: Display genuine enthusiasm for the role and the company. Express your interest in the projects they are working on and how you can contribute. Enthusiasm can leave a positive impression and set you apart from other candidates.
7. **Follow Up**: After the interview, send a thank-you email to the interviewer. Express your appreciation for the opportunity and reiterate your interest in the position. This small gesture can leave a lasting positive impression.

Negotiating the Best Offer

Once you've successfully navigated the interview process and received an offer, it's time to negotiate the best possible terms. Here are some tips for effective negotiation:

1. **Do Your Research**: Before entering negotiations, research the typical salary range for the role, industry standards, and the company's compensation practices. Websites like Glassdoor and Payscale can provide valuable insights.
2. **Know Your Worth**: Understand your value and the unique skills and experiences you bring to the table. Be confident in articulating your worth and how you can contribute to the company's success.
3. **Consider the Entire Package**: Compensation is not just about salary. Consider other aspects of the offer, such as bonuses, stock options, benefits, work-life balance, and opportunities for growth and development. Evaluate the entire package to determine its overall value.
4. **Be Professional and Respectful**: Approach negotiations with professionalism and respect. Express your appreciation for the offer and your enthusiasm for the role. Use positive language and avoid making demands.
5. **Make a Counteroffer**: If the initial offer is not satisfactory, make a counteroffer based on your research and expectations. Be specific about the salary and benefits you are seeking. Provide a rationale for your request, highlighting your skills and market value.
6. **Be Prepared to Compromise**: Negotiation is a two-way process, and compromise may be necessary. Be open to finding a middle ground that satisfies both parties. Consider what aspects of the offer are most important to you and where you are willing to be flexible.
7. **Get Everything in Writing**: Once you reach an agreement, ensure that all terms are documented in writing. This includes salary, benefits, start date, and any other negotiated terms. Having everything in writing helps avoid misunderstandings and ensures clarity.
8. **Know When to Walk Away**: If the offer does not meet your expectations and there is no room for negotiation, be prepared to walk away. It's important to find a role that aligns with your career goals and values. Trust that the right opportunity will come along.

By following these strategies, you can navigate the interview process with confidence and secure the best possible offer. Remember, preparation, practice, and a positive attitude are key to success. Good luck!

Python Basics

Python Syntax and Semantics

Python is known for its simple and readable syntax, which makes it an excellent choice for both beginners and experienced programmers. Understanding Python's syntax and semantics is crucial for writing clean and efficient code.

Syntax refers to the set of rules that define the structure of a Python program. It includes the way code is written, such as indentation, keywords, and operators. **Semantics**, on the other hand, refers to the meaning of the code, or what the code does when it is executed.

Indentation: Unlike many other programming languages that use braces {} to define code blocks, Python uses indentation. This means that the level of indentation determines the grouping of statements. For example:

```
if condition:
    # This block is executed
if the condition is true
    print("Condition is true")
else:
    # This block is executed if
  the condition is false
    print("Condition is false")
```

Comments: Comments are used to explain the code and are ignored by the Python interpreter. Single-line comments start with the # symbol, while multi-line comments are enclosed in triple quotes """.

```
# This is a single-line comment

"""
This is a
multi-line comment
"""
```

Variables and Assignment: Variables in Python are created by assigning a value to a name using the = operator. Python is dynamically typed, meaning you don't need to declare the type of a variable explicitly.

```
x = 10
name = "Alice"
```

Keywords: Python has a set of reserved words, known as keywords, that have special meanings and cannot be used as variable names. Examples include if, else, while, for, def, and return.

Operators: Python supports various operators for arithmetic, comparison, logical, and bitwise operations. For example:

```
# Arithmetic operators
a = 5 + 3    # Addition
b = 10 - 2   # Subtraction
c = 4 * 2    # Multiplication
d = 8 / 2    # Division

# Comparison operators
x = 5
y = 10
print(x == y)   # Equal to
print(x != y)   # Not equal to
print(x < y)    # Less than
print(x > y)    # Greater than

# Logical operators
print(x < y and x != y)
```

```
# Logical AND
print(x < y or x == y)
    # Logical OR
print(not (x < y))
    # Logical NOT
```

Data Types and Variables

Python supports various data types, each serving a different purpose. Understanding these data types and how to use them is fundamental to programming in Python.

Numeric Types: Python has three numeric types: integers, floating-point numbers, and complex numbers.

- **Integers**: Whole numbers without a fractional part. Example: x = 10
- **Floating-point numbers**: Numbers with a fractional part. Example: y = 3.14
- **Complex numbers**: Numbers with a real and imaginary part. Example: z = 2 + 3j

Strings: Strings are sequences of characters enclosed in single quotes ', double quotes ", or triple quotes """. Strings are immutable, meaning they cannot be changed after they are created.

```
name = "Alice"
greeting = 'Hello, world!'
multiline_string = """This is a
multi-line string"""
```

Lists: Lists are ordered collections of items, which can be of different types. Lists are mutable, meaning their contents can be changed.

```
numbers = [1, 2, 3, 4, 5]
mixed_list = [1,
```

```
"Alice", 3.14, True]
numbers.append(6)
# Adding an item to the list
print(numbers[0])
# Accessing the first item
```

Tuples: Tuples are similar to lists but are immutable. Once created, their contents cannot be changed.

```
coordinates = (10, 20)
print(coordinates[0])
# Accessing the first item
```

Dictionaries: Dictionaries are collections of key-value pairs. They are unordered and mutable.

```
person = {"name": "Alice",
"age": 30, "city": "New York"}
print(person["name"])
# Accessing the value associated
with the key "name"
person["age"] = 31
# Changing the value associated with the key "age"
```

Sets: Sets are unordered collections of unique items. They are mutable and do not allow duplicate values.

```
fruits = {"apple", "banana", "cherry"}
fruits.add("orange")
 # Adding an item to the set
print(fruits)
```

Boolean: Boolean values represent True or False. They are often used in conditional statements.

```
is_active = True
print(is_active)
```

Control Structures

Control structures are used to control the flow of execution in a program. Python supports several control structures, including conditional statements, loops, and exception handling.

Conditional Statements: Conditional statements allow you to execute different blocks of code based on certain conditions. The most common conditional statements are if, elif, and else.

```
x = 10
if x > 0:
    print("x is positive")
elif x == 0:
    print("x is zero")
else:
    print("x is negative")
```

Loops: Loops are used to execute a block of code repeatedly. Python supports for loops and while loops.

- **For Loop**: The for loop is used to iterate over a sequence (such as a list, tuple, or string).

```
numbers = [1, 2, 3, 4, 5]
for number in numbers:
    print(number)
```

- **While Loop**: The while loop is used to execute a block of code as long as a condition is true.

```
count = 0
while count < 5:
    print(count)
    count += 1
```

Break and Continue: The break statement is used to exit a loop prematurely, while the continue statement is used to skip the current iteration and continue with the next iteration.

```
for i in range(10):
    if i == 5:
        break
# Exit the loop when i is 5
    print(i)

for i in range(10):
    if i % 2 == 0:
continue  # Skip even numbers
    print(i)
```

Exception Handling: Exception handling is used to handle errors and exceptions that may occur during the execution of a program. The try, except, else, and finally blocks are used for this purpose.

```
try:
    result = 10 / 0
except ZeroDivisionError:
print("Cannot divide by zero")
else:
    print("Division successful")
finally:
print("This block is always executed")
```

Functions and Modules

Functions are reusable blocks of code that perform a specific task. They help in organizing code, making it more readable and maintainable. Python supports both built-in functions and user-defined functions.

Defining Functions: Functions are defined using the def keyword, followed by the function name and parentheses ().

```
def greet(name):
    print(f"Hello, {name}!")

greet("Alice")
```

Return Statement: The return statement is used to return a value from a function.

```
def add(a, b):
    return a + b

result = add(5, 3)
print(result)
```

Default Arguments: Functions can have default arguments, which are used if no value is provided for the argument.

```
def greet(name="Guest"):
print(f"Hello, {name}!")

greet()
greet("Alice")
```

Variable-Length Arguments: Functions can accept a variable number of arguments using *args for positional arguments and **kwargs for keyword arguments.

```
def print_numbers(*args):
for number in args:
print(number)
```

```
print_numbers(1, 2, 3, 4, 5)

def print_info(**kwargs):
for key, value in kwargs.items():
print(f"{key}: {value}")

print_info(name="Alice",
 age=30, city="New York")
```

Lambda Functions: Lambda functions are anonymous functions defined using the lambda keyword. They are often used for short, simple functions.

```
add = lambda a, b: a + b
print(add(5, 3))
```

Modules: Modules are files containing Python code that can be imported and used in other Python programs. They help in organizing code and promoting code reuse.

- **Importing Modules**: Modules can be imported using the import statement.

```
import math
print(math.sqrt(16))
```

- **Importing Specific Functions**: You can import specific functions from a module using the from keyword.

```
from math import sqrt
print(sqrt(16))
```

- **Creating Modules**: You can create your own modules by saving Python code in a .py file and importing it in other programs.

```
# my_module.py
def greet(name):
print(f"Hello, {name}!")

# main.py
import my_module
my_module.greet("Alice")
```

Packages: Packages are collections of modules organized in directories that provide a hierarchical structure. They help in organizing large codebases and promoting code reuse. A package is simply a directory containing an __init__.py file, which can be empty or contain initialization code for the package.

```
# Directory structure
# my_package/
#     __init__.py
#     module1.py
#     module2.py

# module1.py
def function1():
print("Function 1 from module 1")

# module2.py
def function2():
print("Function 2 from module 2")

# main.py
from my_package import module1, module2
```

```
module1.function1()
module2.function2()
```

Standard Library: Python's standard library is a collection of modules and packages that come with Python, providing a wide range of functionalities. Some commonly used modules include os for operating system interactions, sys for system-specific parameters and functions, datetime for date and time manipulation, and json for working with JSON data.

```
import os
import sys
import datetime
import json

# Working with the os module
current_directory = os.getcwd()
print(f"Current Directory:
 {current_directory}")

# Working with the sys module
print(f"Python Version: {sys.version}")

# Working with the datetime module
current_time = datetime.datetime.now()
print(f"Current Time: {current_time}")

# Working with the json module
data = {"name": "Alice", "age": 30}
json_data = json.dumps(data)
print(f"JSON Data: {json_data}")
```

Third-Party Libraries: In addition to the standard library, Python has a vast ecosystem of third-party libraries that can be installed using package managers like pip. These libraries extend Python's capabilities and are widely used in various domains such as web development, data science, machine learning, and more.

```python
# Installing a third-party
library using pip
# pip install requests

import requests

response = requests.get
("https://api.github.com")
print(response.json())
```

Docstrings: Docstrings are used to document functions, classes, and modules. They are enclosed in triple quotes and provide a convenient way to describe the purpose and usage of the code.

```
def add(a, b):
    """
    Add two numbers and return the result.

    Parameters:
a (int): The first number.
b (int): The second number.

    Returns:
int: The sum of the two numbers.
    """
return a + b

print(add.__doc__)
```

List Comprehensions: List comprehensions provide a concise way to create lists. They are often used for creating new lists by applying an expression to each item in an existing list.

```
numbers = [1, 2, 3, 4, 5]
squares =
[x ** 2 for x in numbers]
print(squares)
```

Generators: Generators are a type of iterable, like lists or tuples, but they generate items one at a time and only when needed. They are defined using the yield keyword.

```
def fibonacci(n):
    a, b = 0, 1
    while a < n:
yield a
a, b = b, a + b

for number in fibonacci(10):
    print(number)
```

Decorators: Decorators are a way to modify or extend the behavior of functions or methods. They are defined using the @ symbol and are often used for logging, access control, and memoization.

```
def my_decorator(func):
    def wrapper():
print("Something is happening
before the function is called.")
        func()
print("Something is
happening after the
 function is called.")
    return wrapper

@my_decorator
def say_hello():
    print("Hello!")

say_hello()
```

Context Managers: Context managers are used to manage resources, such as files or network connections, ensuring they are properly acquired and released. They are defined using the with statement.

```python
with open("example.
txt", "w") as file:
file.write("Hello, world!")
```

Classes and Objects: Python supports object-oriented programming (OOP), allowing you to define classes and create objects. Classes are blueprints for creating objects, and objects are instances of classes.

```python
class Person:
def __init__(self, name, age):
self.name = name
self.age = age

    def greet(self):
print(f"Hello, my name is {self.name} and I am {self.age} years old.")

person = Person("Alice", 30)
person.greet()
```

Inheritance: Inheritance allows you to create new classes based on existing ones, promoting code reuse and extensibility.

```python
class Employee(Person):
    def __init__(self,
 name, age, employee_id):
super().__init__(name, age)
self.employee_id = employee_id

    def work(self):
print(f"Employee {self.name} is working.")

employee = Employee
("Bob", 25, "E123")
employee.greet()
```

```
employee.work()
```

Polymorphism: Polymorphism allows you to define methods in a base class and override them in derived classes, enabling different behaviors for the same method.

```
class Animal:
    def speak(self):
        pass

class Dog(Animal):
    def speak(self):
        return "Woof!"

class Cat(Animal):
def speak(self):
return "Meow!"

animals = [Dog(), Cat()]
for animal in animals:
print(animal.speak())
```

Encapsulation: Encapsulation is the practice of hiding the internal state and behavior of an object, exposing only what is necessary. This is achieved using private and protected attributes.

```
class BankAccount:
    def __init__(self, balance):
self.__balance =
balance   # Private attribute

    def deposit(self, amount):
self.__balance += amount

    def withdraw(self, amount):
if amount <= self.__balance:
self.__balance -= amount
```

```
        else:
print("Insufficient funds")

    def get_balance(self):
        return self.__balance

account = BankAccount(1000)
account.deposit(500)
account.withdraw(200)
print(account.get_balance())
```

Abstract Classes and Interfaces: Abstract classes and interfaces define methods that must be implemented by derived classes. They are used to create a common interface for different implementations.

```
from abc import ABC, abstractmethod

class Shape(ABC):
    @abstractmethod
    def area(self):
        pass

class Rectangle(Shape):
def __init__(self, width, height):
self.width = width
self.height = height

    def area(self):
return self.width * self.height

rectangle = Rectangle(10, 20)
print(rectangle.area())
```

File Handling: Python provides built-in functions for working with files, allowing you to read from and write to files.

```python
# Writing to a file
with open("example.txt",
 "w") as file:
    file.write("Hello, world!")

# Reading from a file
with open("example.txt", "r") as file:
    content = file.read()
    print(content)
```

Regular Expressions: Regular expressions are used for pattern matching and text manipulation. The re module provides functions for working with regular expressions.

```python
import re

pattern = r"\b[A-Za-z]+\b"
text = "Hello, world! Welcome to Python programming."

matches = re.findall(pattern, text)
print(matches)
```

Unit Testing: Unit testing is the practice of testing individual units of code to ensure they work as expected. The unittest module provides a framework for writing and running tests.

```python
import unittest

def add(a, b):
    return a + b

class TestAddFunction(unittest.TestCase):
    def test_add(self):
        self.assertEqual(add(2, 3), 5)
        self.assertEqual(add(-1, 1), 0)
```

```python
if __name__ == "__main__":
    unittest.main()
```

Debugging: Debugging is the process of identifying and fixing errors in code. Python provides tools like pdb for interactive debugging.

```python
import pdb

def faulty_function():
    x = 10
    y = 0
    pdb.set_trace()  # Set a breakpoint
    result = x / y
    return result

faulty_function()
```

Logging: Logging is used to record information about the execution of a program, which can be helpful for debugging and monitoring. The logging module provides a flexible framework for logging.

```python
import logging

logging.basicConfig(level=logging.INFO)
logger = logging.getLogger(__name__)

def divide(a, b):
    try:
        result = a / b
        logger.info(f"Division successful: {result}")
        return result
    except ZeroDivisionError:
        logger.error("Cannot divide by zero")
        return None

divide(10, 2)
divide(10, 0)
```

By mastering these Python basics, you will have a solid foundation for tackling more advanced topics and solving complex problems. Python's simplicity and versatility make it an ideal language for programming interviews, allowing you to focus on demonstrating your problem-solving skills and technical knowledge.

Data Structures

Arrays and Lists

Arrays and **lists** are fundamental data structures used to store collections of elements. While they are similar, there are key differences between them.

Arrays: Arrays are a collection of elements, typically of the same data type, stored in contiguous memory locations. They allow for efficient indexing and iteration. In Python, arrays can be created using the array module, but lists are more commonly used due to their flexibility.

```
import array

# Creating an array of integers
arr = array.array('i', [1, 2, 3, 4, 5])
print(arr[0])  # Accessing the first element
```

Lists: Lists are dynamic arrays that can store elements of different data types. They are mutable, meaning their contents can be changed. Lists provide various methods for adding, removing, and manipulating elements.

```
# Creating a list
numbers = [1, 2, 3, 4, 5]
print(numbers[0])  # Accessing the first element

# Adding elements
numbers.append(6)
```

```
numbers.insert(0, 0)

# Removing elements
numbers.remove(3)
numbers.pop()

# Slicing
print(numbers[1:4])  # Accessing a sublist
```

Lists are versatile and widely used in Python due to their ease of use and built-in methods.

Linked Lists

Linked lists are linear data structures where elements, called nodes, are linked using pointers. Each node contains two parts: the data and a reference to the next node in the sequence. Linked lists are dynamic and can grow or shrink in size.

Singly Linked List: In a singly linked list, each node points to the next node.

```
class Node:
    def __init__(self, data):
        self.data = data
        self.next = None

class SinglyLinkedList:
    def __init__(self):
        self.head = None

    def append(self, data):
        new_node = Node(data)
        if not self.head:
            self.head = new_node
            return
        last = self.head
        while last.next:
            last = last.next
        last.next = new_node
```

```python
    def print_list(self):
        current = self.head
        while current:
            print(current.data, end=" -> ")
            current = current.next
        print("None")

# Creating a singly linked list
sll = SinglyLinkedList()
sll.append(1)
sll.append(2)
sll.append(3)
sll.print_list()
```

Doubly Linked List: In a doubly linked list, each node points to both the next and the previous node.

```python
class Node:
    def __init__(self, data):
        self.data = data
        self.next = None
        self.prev = None

class DoublyLinkedList:
    def __init__(self):
        self.head = None

    def append(self, data):
        new_node = Node(data)
        if not self.head:
            self.head = new_node
            return
        last = self.head
        while last.next:
            last = last.next
        last.next = new_node
        new_node.prev = last
```

```python
    def print_list(self):
        current = self.head
        while current:
            print(current.data, end=" <-> ")
            current = current.next
        print("None")

# Creating a doubly linked list
dll = DoublyLinkedList()
dll.append(1)
dll.append(2)
dll.append(3)
dll.print_list()
```

Linked lists are useful for dynamic memory allocation and efficient insertion and deletion of elements.

Stacks and Queues

Stacks and **queues** are linear data structures that follow specific order principles for adding and removing elements.

Stacks: A stack follows the Last In, First Out (LIFO) principle. Elements are added and removed from the top of the stack.

```python
class Stack:
    def __init__(self):
        self.stack = []

    def push(self, data):
        self.stack.append(data)

    def pop(self):
        if not self.is_empty():
            return self.stack.pop()
        return None

    def peek(self):
        if not self.is_empty():
```

DATA STRUCTURES

```python
        return self.stack[-1]
    return None

def is_empty(self):
    return len(self.stack) == 0

# Using a stack
stack = Stack()
stack.push(1)
stack.push(2)
stack.push(3)
print(stack.pop())   # Output: 3
print(stack.peek())  # Output: 2
```

Queues: A queue follows the First In, First Out (FIFO) principle. Elements are added at the rear and removed from the front.

```python
class Queue:
    def __init__(self):
        self.queue = []

    def enqueue(self, data):
        self.queue.append(data)

    def dequeue(self):
        if not self.is_empty():
            return self.queue.pop(0)
        return None

    def peek(self):
        if not self.is_empty():
            return self.queue[0]
        return None

    def is_empty(self):
        return len(self.queue) == 0

# Using a queue
```

```python
queue = Queue()
queue.enqueue(1)
queue.enqueue(2)
queue.enqueue(3)
print(queue.dequeue())  # Output: 1
print(queue.peek())     # Output: 2
```

Stacks and queues are used in various applications, such as expression evaluation, backtracking, and task scheduling.

Hash Tables

Hash tables are data structures that store key-value pairs. They use a hash function to compute an index into an array of buckets or slots, from which the desired value can be found.

```python
class HashTable:
    def __init__(self):
        self.size = 10
        self.table = [[] for _ in range(self.size)]

    def hash_function(self, key):
        return hash(key) % self.size

    def insert(self, key, value):
        index = self.hash_function(key)
        for kvp in self.table[index]:
            if kvp[0] == key:
                kvp[1] = value
                return
        self.table[index].append([key, value])

    def get(self, key):
        index = self.hash_function(key)
        for kvp in self.table[index]:
            if kvp[0] == key:
                return kvp[1]
        return None

    def remove(self, key):
```

```
        index = self.hash_function(key)
        for kvp in self.table[index]:
            if kvp[0] == key:
                self.table[index].remove(kvp)
                return

# Using a hash table
ht = HashTable()
ht.insert("name", "Alice")
ht.insert("age", 30)
print(ht.get("name"))  # Output: Alice
ht.remove("age")
print(ht.get("age"))   # Output: None
```

Hash tables provide efficient insertion, deletion, and lookup operations, making them ideal for implementing associative arrays, databases, and caches.

Trees and Graphs

Trees and **graphs** are hierarchical data structures used to represent relationships between elements.

Trees: A tree is a collection of nodes connected by edges, with a single root node and no cycles. The most common type of tree is the binary tree, where each node has at most two children.

```
class TreeNode:
    def __init__(self, data):
        self.data = data
        self.left = None
        self.right = None

class BinaryTree:
    def __init__(self):
        self.root = None

    def insert(self, data):
        if not self.root:
            self.root = TreeNode(data)
        else:
```

```python
            self._insert(self.root, data)

    def _insert(self, node, data):
        if data < node.data:
            if node.left:
                self._insert(node.left, data)
            else:
                node.left = TreeNode(data)
        else:
            if node.right:
                self._insert(node.right, data)
            else:
                node.right = TreeNode(data)

    def inorder_traversal(self, node):
        if node:
            self.inorder_traversal(node.left)
            print(node.data, end=" ")
            self.inorder_traversal(node.right)

# Using a binary tree
bt = BinaryTree()
bt.insert(10)
bt.insert(5)
bt.insert(15)
bt.inorder_traversal(bt.root)  # Output: 5 10 15
```

Graphs: A graph is a collection of nodes (vertices) connected by edges. Graphs can be directed or undirected, and they can contain cycles.

```python
class Graph:
    def __init__(self):
        self.graph = {}

    def add_edge(self, u, v):
        if u not in self.graph:
            self.graph[u] = []
        self.graph[u].append(v)
```

```python
    def bfs(self, start):
        visited = set()
        queue = [start]
        while queue:
            vertex = queue.pop(0)
            if vertex not in visited:
                print(vertex, end=" ")
                visited.add(vertex)
                queue.extend(self.graph.get(vertex, []))

# Using a graph
g = Graph()
g.add_edge(1, 2)
g.add_edge(1, 3)
g.add_edge(2, 4)
g.add_edge(3, 4)
g.bfs(1)   # Output: 1 2 3 4
```

Trees and graphs are used in various applications, such as representing hierarchical data, network routing, and social networks.

Heaps and Priority Queues

Heaps are specialized tree-based data structures that satisfy the heap property. In a max heap, for any given node i, the value of i is greater than or equal to the values of its children. In a min heap, the value of i is less than or equal to the values of its children. Heaps are commonly used to implement priority queues.

Max Heap: In a max heap, the largest element is at the root.

```python
import heapq

# Creating a max heap
class MaxHeap:
    def __init__(self):
        self.heap = []

    def push(self, item):
        heapq.heappush(self.heap, -item)
```

```python
    def pop(self):
        return -heapq.heappop(self.heap)

    def peek(self):
        return -self.heap[0]

# Using a max heap
max_heap = MaxHeap()
max_heap.push(10)
max_heap.push(20)
max_heap.push(5)
print(max_heap.pop())   # Output: 20
print(max_heap.peek())  # Output: 10
```

Min Heap: In a min heap, the smallest element is at the root.

```python
# Creating a min heap
min_heap = []
heapq.heappush(min_heap, 10)
heapq.heappush(min_heap, 20)
heapq.heappush(min_heap, 5)
print(heapq.heappop(min_heap))  # Output: 5
print(min_heap[0])  # Output: 10
```

Priority Queues: Priority queues are abstract data types where each element has a priority. Elements with higher priority are dequeued before elements with lower priority. Heaps are often used to implement priority queues due to their efficient insertion and extraction operations.

```python
class PriorityQueue:
    def __init__(self):
        self.queue = []

    def push(self, item, priority):
        heapq.heappush(self.queue, (priority, item))
```

```python
    def pop(self):
        return heapq.heappop(self.queue)[1]

    def peek(self):
        return self.queue[0][1]

# Using a priority queue
pq = PriorityQueue()
pq.push("task1", 2)
pq.push("task2", 1)
pq.push("task3", 3)
print(pq.pop())    # Output: task2
print(pq.peek())   # Output: task1
```

Heaps and priority queues are used in various applications, such as scheduling algorithms, Dijkstra's shortest path algorithm, and Huffman coding.

Summary

Understanding and mastering these fundamental data structures—arrays and lists, linked lists, stacks and queues, hash tables, trees and graphs, and heaps and priority queues—is crucial for solving a wide range of programming problems. Each data structure has its own strengths and weaknesses, and knowing when and how to use them will greatly enhance your problem-solving skills and performance in programming interviews. By practicing and implementing these data structures in Python, you will be well-prepared to tackle any coding challenge that comes your way.

Algorithms

Sorting Algorithms
Sorting algorithms are fundamental in computer science, used to rearrange elements in a list or array into a specific order, typically ascending or descending. Here are some common sorting algorithms:

1. Bubble Sort: This is a simple comparison-based algorithm where each pair of adjacent elements is compared, and the elements are swapped if they are in the wrong order. This process is repeated until the list is sorted. Although easy to understand, bubble sort is inefficient for large datasets with a time complexity of
$O(n2)$
.

2. Selection Sort: This algorithm divides the list into two parts: the sorted part and the unsorted part. It repeatedly selects the smallest (or largest) element from the unsorted part and moves it to the end of the sorted part. Like bubble sort, it has a time complexity of
$O(n2)$
.

3. Insertion Sort: This algorithm builds the sorted list one element at a time by repeatedly taking the next element from the unsorted part and inserting it into the correct position in the sorted part. It is efficient for small datasets or nearly sorted data, with a time complexity of
$O(n2)$

in the worst case but
$O(n)$
in the best case.

4. Merge Sort: This is a divide-and-conquer algorithm that divides the list into two halves, recursively sorts each half, and then merges the sorted halves to produce the final sorted list. Merge sort has a time complexity of
$O(n \log n)$
and is stable, but it requires additional space for the temporary arrays used during merging.

5. Quick Sort: Another divide-and-conquer algorithm, quick sort selects a 'pivot' element and partitions the list into two sublists: elements less than the pivot and elements greater than the pivot. It then recursively sorts the sublists. Quick sort has an average time complexity of
$O(n \log n)$
but can degrade to
$O(n^2)$
in the worst case if the pivot selection is poor.

6. Heap Sort: This algorithm uses a binary heap data structure to sort elements. It first builds a max heap from the input data, then repeatedly extracts the maximum element from the heap and rebuilds the heap until all elements are sorted. Heap sort has a time complexity of
$O(n \log n)$
and is not stable.

Searching Algorithms
Searching algorithms are used to find specific elements within a data structure. Here are some common searching algorithms:

1. Linear Search: This is the simplest searching algorithm, where each element in the list is checked sequentially until the desired element is found or the list is exhausted. Linear search has a time complexity of

O(n)

2. Binary Search: This algorithm is used on sorted lists. It repeatedly divides the search interval in half, comparing the target value to the middle element of the list. If the target value is less than the middle element, the search continues in the lower half; otherwise, it continues in the upper half. Binary search has a time complexity of
O(logn)

3. Interpolation Search: This algorithm is an improvement over binary search for uniformly distributed data. It estimates the position of the target value based on the values at the ends of the search interval. Interpolation search has a time complexity of
O(loglogn)
in the best case but can degrade to
O(n)
in the worst case.

Recursion and Backtracking

Recursion is a technique where a function calls itself to solve smaller instances of the same problem. It is often used in problems that can be broken down into smaller, similar subproblems. Recursion can simplify code and make it more readable, but it can also lead to high memory usage and stack overflow if not used carefully.

Backtracking is a refinement of recursion where the algorithm tries to build a solution incrementally, removing those solutions that fail to satisfy the constraints of the problem at any point. It is used in problems like solving puzzles, finding paths in a maze, and generating permutations. Backtracking is often implemented using recursion.

Example of backtracking: Solving the N-Queens problem, where the goal is to place N queens on an N×N chessboard such that no two queens threaten each other.

```
def solve_n_queens(n):
    def is_safe(board, row, col):
        for i in range(row):
            if board[i] == col or \
               board[i] - i == col - row or \
               board[i] + i == col + row:
                return False
        return True

    def solve(board, row):
        if row == n:
            result.append(board[:])
            return
        for col in range(n):
            if is_safe(board, row, col):
                board[row] = col
                solve(board, row + 1)
                board[row] = -1

    result = []
    solve([-1] * n, 0)
    return result

print(solve_n_queens(4))
```

Dynamic Programming

Dynamic Programming (DP) is a method for solving complex problems by breaking them down into simpler subproblems. It is used when the problem can be divided into overlapping subproblems that can be solved independently. DP stores the results of subproblems to avoid redundant computations, making it more efficient.

There are two main approaches to DP:

1. **Top-Down Approach (Memoization)**: This approach involves solving the problem recursively and storing the results of subproblems in a table to avoid redundant computations.

2. **Bottom-Up Approach (Tabulation)**: This approach involves solving the subproblems iteratively and building up the solution to the main problem from the solutions of the subproblems.

Example: Solving the Fibonacci sequence using DP.

```
def fibonacci(n):
    if n <= 1:
        return n
    dp = [0] * (n + 1)
    dp[1] = 1
    for i in range(2, n + 1):
        dp[i] = dp[i - 1] + dp[i - 2]
    return dp[n]

print(fibonacci(10))
```

Greedy Algorithms

Greedy algorithms are used to solve optimization problems by making a sequence of choices, each of which looks best at the moment. The algorithm makes a locally optimal choice at each step with the hope of finding a global optimum.

Example: The **Activity Selection Problem**, where the goal is to select the maximum number of activities that don't overlap.

```
def activity_selection(activities):
    activities.sort(key=lambda x: x[1])
    selected_activities = [activities[0]]
    last_end_time = activities[0][1]
    for i in range(1, len(activities)):
        if activities[i][0] >= last_end_time:
            selected_activities.append(activities[i])
            last_end_time = activities[i][1]
    return selected_activities

activities = [(1, 3), (2, 5), (4, 6), (6, 7), (5, 8)]
```

```
print(activity_selection(activities))
```

Graph Algorithms

Graph algorithms are used to solve problems related to graph data structures, which consist of nodes (vertices) and edges connecting them. Common graph algorithms include:

1. **Depth-First Search (DFS)**: This algorithm explores as far as possible along each branch before backtracking.

6. **Bellman-Ford Algorithm**: This algorithm computes the shortest paths from a single source vertex to all other vertices in a weighted graph. Unlike Dijkstra's algorithm, Bellman-Ford can handle graphs with negative weight edges. It works by repeatedly relaxing all the edges, ensuring that the shortest path is found even if there are negative weight cycles. The time complexity is
$$O(VE)$$
, where
$$V$$
is the number of vertices and
$$E$$
is the number of edges.

7. **Floyd-Warshall Algorithm**: This algorithm finds the shortest paths between all pairs of vertices in a weighted graph. It uses a dynamic programming approach to iteratively improve the estimate of the shortest path between any two vertices. The time complexity is
$$O(V3)$$
, making it suitable for smaller graphs.

8. **Topological Sorting**: This algorithm is used for ordering the vertices of a directed acyclic graph (DAG) such that for every directed edge
$$uv$$
from vertex
$$u$$
to vertex

u comes before v in the ordering. It is useful in scenarios like task scheduling and resolving dependencies. The time complexity is O(V+E).

9. **Tarjan's Algorithm**: This algorithm finds all strongly connected components (SCCs) in a directed graph. An SCC is a maximal subgraph where every vertex is reachable from every other vertex in the subgraph. Tarjan's algorithm uses depth-first search (DFS) and has a time complexity of O(V+E).

10. A Search Algorithm*: This is a pathfinding and graph traversal algorithm used in many applications, such as games and navigation systems. It uses heuristics to guide the search, combining the benefits of Dijkstra's algorithm and greedy best-first search. The time complexity depends on the heuristic used but is generally efficient for practical purposes.

Summary

Understanding and mastering these algorithms—sorting, searching, recursion and backtracking, dynamic programming, greedy algorithms, and graph algorithms—are essential for solving a wide range of computational problems efficiently and effectively. Each algorithm has its own strengths and weaknesses, and knowing when and how to use them will greatly enhance your problem-solving skills and performance in programming interviews. By practicing and implementing these algorithms in Python, you will be well-prepared to tackle any coding challenge that comes your way.

Advanced Topics

Concurrency and Parallelism

Concurrency and **parallelism** are key concepts in modern computing, enabling efficient execution of multiple tasks. While they are often used interchangeably, they have distinct meanings.

Concurrency: Concurrency involves multiple tasks making progress simultaneously. It doesn't necessarily mean that tasks are running at the same time, but rather that they are managed in such a way that they appear to be. This is achieved through techniques like context switching, where the CPU switches between tasks, giving the illusion of parallel execution. Concurrency is essential for improving the responsiveness of applications, especially in environments where tasks are I/O-bound.

Parallelism: Parallelism, on the other hand, involves the simultaneous execution of multiple tasks. This is typically achieved using multiple processors or cores. Parallelism is about dividing a task into smaller sub-tasks that can be processed simultaneously, thus speeding up computation. It is particularly useful for CPU-bound tasks that require significant processing power.

Example: In Python, concurrency can be achieved using the threading module, while parallelism can be implemented using the multiprocessing module.

```
import threading
import multiprocessing
```

```python
# Concurrency with threading
def print_numbers():
    for i in range(5):
        print(i)

thread = threading.Thread(target=print_numbers)
thread.start()

# Parallelism with multiprocessing
def square_number(n):
    return n * n

if __name__ == "__main__":
    with multiprocessing.Pool() as pool:
        result = pool.map(square_number, [1, 2, 3, 4, 5])
        print(result)
```

Concurrency and parallelism are crucial for building efficient, high-performance applications, especially in fields like data processing, web development, and scientific computing[12].

Design Patterns

Design patterns are reusable solutions to common problems in software design. They provide a standard terminology and are specific to particular scenarios. Design patterns can be categorized into three main types:

1. **Creational Patterns**: These patterns deal with object creation mechanisms, trying to create objects in a manner suitable to the situation. Examples include the Singleton, Factory, and Builder patterns.
2. **Structural Patterns**: These patterns deal with object composition, ensuring that if one part changes, the entire structure doesn't need to change. Examples include Adapter, Composite, and Decorator patterns.
3. **Behavioral Patterns**: These patterns deal with object interaction and responsibility. Examples include Observer, Strategy, and Command patterns.

ADVANCED TOPICS

Example: The Singleton pattern ensures a class has only one instance and provides a global point of access to it.

```
class Singleton:
    _instance = None

    def __new__(cls):
        if cls._instance is None:
            cls._instance = super(Singleton, cls).__new__(cls)
        return cls._instance

singleton1 = Singleton()
singleton2 = Singleton()
print(singleton1 is singleton2)  # Output: True
```

Design patterns help in creating more robust, maintainable, and scalable software systems[34].

Object-Oriented Programming

Object-Oriented Programming (OOP) is a programming paradigm based on the concept of objects, which can contain data and code. The four main principles of OOP are:

1. **Encapsulation**: This principle states that all data and methods should be bundled within an object. It restricts direct access to some of the object's components, which can prevent the accidental modification of data.
2. **Abstraction**: Abstraction means hiding the complex implementation details and showing only the necessary features of an object. It helps in reducing programming complexity and effort.
3. **Inheritance**: Inheritance allows a new class to inherit the properties and methods of an existing class. This promotes code reusability and establishes a natural hierarchy between classes.
4. **Polymorphism**: Polymorphism allows objects to be treated as instances of their parent class rather than their actual class. It enables a single interface to represent different underlying forms (data types).

Example: Implementing a simple class hierarchy in Python.

```
class Animal:
    def speak(self):
        raise NotImplementedError("Subclass must implement
        abstract method")

class Dog(Animal):
    def speak(self):
        return "Woof!"

class Cat(Animal):
    def speak(self):
        return "Meow!"

animals = [Dog(), Cat()]
for animal in animals:
    print(animal.speak())
```

OOP helps in organizing code in a more modular and reusable way, making it easier to manage and maintain[56].

Functional Programming

Functional Programming (FP) is a programming paradigm where programs are constructed by applying and composing functions. It emphasizes the use of pure functions, immutability, and higher-order functions.

Pure Functions: A pure function is a function that, given the same input, will always return the same output and does not have any side effects (e.g., modifying a global variable).

Immutability: In FP, data is immutable, meaning it cannot be changed once created. Instead, new data structures are created from existing ones.

Higher-Order Functions: These are functions that take other functions as arguments or return them as results.

Example: Implementing a simple functional program in Python.

ADVANCED TOPICS

```python
from functools import reduce

# Pure function
def add(x, y):
    return x + y

# Higher-order function
def apply_function(func, x, y):
    return func(x, y)

# Using map, filter, and reduce
numbers = [1, 2, 3, 4, 5]
squared = list(map(lambda x: x * x, numbers))
even = list(filter(lambda x: x % 2 == 0, numbers))
sum_of_numbers = reduce(add, numbers)

print(squared)         # Output: [1, 4, 9, 16, 25]
print(even)            # Output: [2, 4]
print(sum_of_numbers)  # Output: 15
```

FP promotes a declarative coding style, making code more predictable and easier to test[78].

Memory Management and Optimization

Memory management is a crucial aspect of programming, involving the allocation, use, and release of memory in an efficient manner. Proper memory management ensures that applications run smoothly without consuming excessive resources.

Garbage Collection: In languages like Python, garbage collection is used to automatically reclaim memory by tracking and disposing of objects that are no longer in use.

Manual Memory Management: In languages like C and C++, developers must manually allocate and deallocate memory using functions like malloc and free.

Memory Optimization Techniques:

- **Avoiding Memory Leaks**: Ensure that all allocated memory is properly

deallocated.
- **Using Efficient Data Structures**: Choose data structures that use memory efficiently. For example, using arrays instead of linked lists can save memory.
- **Minimizing Object Creation**: Reuse objects instead of creating new ones whenever possible.
- **Profiling and Monitoring**: Use tools to profile memory usage and identify bottlenecks.

Example: Using Python's gc module to manage garbage collection.

```
import gc

# Enable automatic garbage collection
gc.enable()

# Disable automatic garbage collection
gc.disable()

# Manually trigger garbage collection
gc.collect()
```

Effective memory management and optimization are essential for building high-performance applications, especially in resource-constrained environments [9][10].

By mastering these advanced topics—concurrency and parallelism, design patterns, object-oriented programming, functional programming, and memory management and optimization—you will be well-equipped to tackle complex programming challenges and develop efficient, maintainable, and scalable software solutions.

Coding Problems

A rray and String Problems

Array and string problems are fundamental in programming interviews. They test your understanding of data manipulation, indexing, and efficient algorithm design.

1. Array Problems:

- **Find the Minimum and Maximum Element**: Given an array, find the smallest and largest elements.
- **Kth Largest and Smallest Element**: Find the Kth largest and smallest elements in an array.
- **Subarray with Given Sum**: Find a subarray that sums to a given value.
- **Move All Zeroes to End**: Rearrange the array so that all zeroes are at the end while maintaining the order of other elements.
- **Rotate Array**: Rotate the array to the right by a given number of steps.

Example: Finding the Kth largest element using a heap.

```
import heapq

def find_kth_largest(nums, k):
    return heapq.nlargest(k, nums)[-1]

nums = [3, 2, 1, 5, 6, 4]
k = 2
print(find_kth_largest(nums, k))  # Output: 5
```

2. String Problems:

- **Reverse a String**: Reverse the characters in a string.
- **Check for Anagrams**: Determine if two strings are anagrams of each other.
- **Longest Substring Without Repeating Characters**: Find the length of the longest substring without repeating characters.
- **Palindrome Check**: Check if a string is a palindrome.
- **String Compression**: Compress a string using the counts of repeated characters.

Example: Checking for anagrams using a character count.

```
def is_anagram(s1, s2):
    return sorted(s1) == sorted(s2)

s1 = "listen"
s2 = "silent"
print(is_anagram(s1, s2))  # Output: True
```

Linked List Problems

Linked lists are linear data structures where elements are stored in nodes, with each node pointing to the next. They are useful for dynamic memory allocation and efficient insertions/deletions.

1. Reverse a Linked List: Reverse the nodes of a linked list. **2. Detect a Cycle**: Determine if a linked list has a cycle. **3. Merge Two Sorted Lists**: Merge two sorted linked lists into one sorted list. **4. Remove Nth Node from End**: Remove the Nth node from the end of the list. **5. Find Intersection Point**: Find the intersection point of two linked lists.

Example: Reversing a linked list.

```
class ListNode:
    def __init__(self, val=0, next=None):
```

CODING PROBLEMS

```python
        self.val = val
        self.next = next

def reverse_list(head):
    prev = None
    current = head
    while current:
        next_node = current.next
        current.next = prev
        prev = current
        current = next_node
    return prev

# Creating a linked list 1 -> 2 -> 3 -> 4 -> 5
head = ListNode(1, ListNode(2, ListNode(3, ListNode(4, ListNode(5)))))
reversed_head = reverse_list(head)
```

Stack and Queue Problems

Stacks and **queues** are linear data structures that follow specific order principles. Stacks follow Last In First Out (LIFO), while queues follow First In First Out (FIFO).

1. Stack Problems:

- **Valid Parentheses**: Check if a string of parentheses is valid.
- **Min Stack**: Design a stack that supports push, pop, and retrieving the minimum element in constant time.
- **Evaluate Reverse Polish Notation**: Evaluate the value of an arithmetic expression in Reverse Polish Notation.

Example: Validating parentheses using a stack.

```python
def is_valid_parentheses(s):
    stack = []
    mapping = {")": "(", "}": "{", "]": "["}
    for char in s:
```

```python
        if char in mapping:
            top_element = stack.pop() if stack else '#'
            if mapping[char] != top_element:
                return False
        else:
            stack.append(char)
    return not stack

s = "()[]{}"
print(is_valid_parentheses(s))   # Output: True
```

2. **Queue Problems**:

- **Implement Queue using Stacks**: Implement a queue using two stacks.
- **Circular Queue**: Design a circular queue.
- **Sliding Window Maximum**: Find the maximum value in each sliding window of size k.

Example: Implementing a queue using two stacks.

```python
class MyQueue:
    def __init__(self):
        self.stack1 = []
        self.stack2 = []

    def push(self, x):
        self.stack1.append(x)

    def pop(self):
        if not self.stack2:
            while self.stack1:
                self.stack2.append(self.stack1.pop())
        return self.stack2.pop()

    def peek(self):
        if not self.stack2:
```

```
        while self.stack1:
            self.stack2.append(self.stack1.pop())
    return self.stack2[-1]

def empty(self):
    return not self.stack1 and not self.stack2

queue = MyQueue()
queue.push(1)
queue.push(2)
print(queue.peek())   # Output: 1
print(queue.pop())    # Output: 1
print(queue.empty())  # Output: False
```

Tree and Graph Problems

Trees and **graphs** are non-linear data structures used to represent hierarchical and networked relationships.

1. Tree Problems:

- **Binary Tree Inorder Traversal**: Traverse a binary tree in inorder.
- **Lowest Common Ancestor**: Find the lowest common ancestor of two nodes in a binary tree.
- **Serialize and Deserialize Binary Tree**: Convert a binary tree to a string and back.

Example: Inorder traversal of a binary tree.

```
class TreeNode:
    def __init__(self, val=0, left=None, right=None):
        self.val = val
        self.left = left
        self.right = right

def inorder_traversal(root):
    result = []
    def traverse(node):
```

```
        if node:
            traverse(node.left)
            result.append(node.val)
            traverse(node.right)
    traverse(root)
    return result

# Creating a binary tree 1 -> 2 -> 3
root = TreeNode(1, TreeNode(2), TreeNode(3))
print(inorder_traversal(root))  # Output: [2, 1, 3]
```

2. Graph Problems:

- **Depth-First Search (DFS)**: Traverse a graph using DFS.
- **Breadth-First Search (BFS)**: Traverse a graph using BFS.
- **Dijkstra's Algorithm**: Find the shortest path in a weighted graph.

Example: Depth-First Search in a graph.

```
def dfs(graph, start, visited=None):
    if visited is None:
        visited = set()
    visited.add(start)
    print(start)
    for next in graph[start] - visited:
        dfs(graph, next, visited)
    return visited

graph = {
    'A': {'B', 'C'},
    'B': {'A', 'D', 'E'},
    'C': {'A', 'F'},
    'D': {'B'},
    'E': {'B', 'F'},
    'F': {'C', 'E'}
}
dfs(graph, 'A')
```

Dynamic Programming Problems

Dynamic Programming (DP) is a method for solving complex problems by breaking them down into simpler subproblems and storing the results to avoid redundant computations.

1. Fibonacci Sequence: Compute the nth Fibonacci number. **2. Longest Common Subsequence**: Find the longest subsequence common to two strings. **3. 0/1 Knapsack Problem**: Maximize the value of items that can be placed in a knapsack with a given capacity.

Example: Solving the 0/1 Knapsack problem using DP.

```
def knapsack(weights, values, capacity):
    n = len(weights)
    dp = [[0 for _ in range(capacity + 1)] for _ in range(n + 1)]
    for i in range(1, n + 1):
        for w in range(1, capacity + 1):
            if weights[i - 1] <= w:
                dp[i][w] = max(dp[i - 1][w], dp[i - 1][w - weights[i - 1]] + values[i - 1])
            else:
                dp[i][w] = dp[i - 1][w]
    return dp[n][capacity]

weights = [1, 2, 3]
values = [10, 15, 40]
capacity = 5
print(knapsack(weights, values, capacity))  # Output: 55
```

Miscellaneous Problems

Miscellaneous problems cover a wide range of topics and often require a combination of different techniques and data structures.

1. Bit Manipulation: Perform operations on binary representations of numbers. **2. Regular Expressions**: Use regex to match patterns in strings. **3. Game Theory**: Solve problems related to optimal strategies in games. **4. Geometry**: Solve problems involving geometric shapes and properties. **5. Mathematical Problems**: Solve problems involving number theory, combinatorics, and algebra.

Example: Counting the number of 1s in the binary representation of a number.

```
def count_ones(n):
    count = 0
    while n:
        n &= (n - 1)
        count += 1
    return count

n =
```

System Design

Basics of System Design

System design is the process of defining the architecture, components, modules, interfaces, and data for a system to satisfy specified requirements. It involves translating user requirements into a detailed blueprint that guides the implementation phase. Here are the key steps involved in system design:

1. **Understanding Requirements**: Before starting the design process, it's crucial to gather and understand the requirements. This includes functional requirements (what the system should do) and non-functional requirements (performance, scalability, security, etc.).
2. **High-Level Design (HLD)**: This involves creating a broad overview of the system architecture. It includes identifying the major components, their interactions, and the technologies to be used. HLD focuses on the system's structure and how it will meet the requirements.
3. **Low-Level Design (LLD)**: This is a more detailed design phase where each component is described in detail. It includes data structures, algorithms, and the flow of data between components. LLD ensures that each part of the system is well-defined and can be implemented effectively.
4. **Defining Interfaces**: Interfaces between different components must be clearly defined. This includes APIs, protocols, and data formats. Well-defined interfaces ensure that components can interact seamlessly.
5. **Data Modeling**: Designing the data model involves defining the schema

for databases, the structure of data files, and the data flow between components. This step is crucial for ensuring data integrity and efficient data management.
6. **Scalability and Performance Considerations**: The design must consider how the system will handle increased load and data volume. This includes strategies for load balancing, caching, and database optimization.
7. **Testing and Validation**: The design should be validated by testing the system with realistic data and use cases. This helps identify and address any issues before implementation.
8. **Deployment and Maintenance**: Finally, the system is deployed and maintained over time. This includes fixing bugs, updating components, and adding new features as needed[12].

Designing Scalable Systems

Scalability is the ability of a system to handle a growing amount of work or its potential to accommodate growth. Designing scalable systems is crucial for ensuring that applications can handle increased traffic and data without compromising performance or reliability. Here are some key principles and techniques for designing scalable systems:

1. **Horizontal and Vertical Scaling**:

- **Vertical Scaling**: Adding more resources (CPU, memory, storage) to a single server. This is simpler but has limitations due to hardware constraints.
- **Horizontal Scaling**: Adding more servers to distribute the load. This approach is more flexible and can handle larger increases in traffic and data.

1. **Load Balancing**: Distributing incoming requests evenly across multiple servers to prevent any single server from becoming a bottleneck. Load balancers can be hardware-based or software-based.

2. **Caching**: Storing frequently accessed data in a cache to reduce the load on the database and improve response times. Caching can be implemented at various levels, including client-side, server-side, and database caching.
3. **Database Sharding**: Splitting a large database into smaller, more manageable pieces called shards. Each shard is stored on a separate server, allowing for parallel processing and improved performance.
4. **Replication**: Creating copies of data on multiple servers to ensure high availability and fault tolerance. Replication can be synchronous (real-time) or asynchronous (delayed).
5. **Microservices Architecture**: Breaking down a monolithic application into smaller, independent services that can be developed, deployed, and scaled independently. This approach improves flexibility and scalability.
6. **Asynchronous Processing**: Using message queues and background processing to handle tasks that don't need immediate responses. This helps in managing high loads and improving system responsiveness.
7. **Monitoring and Auto-Scaling**: Implementing monitoring tools to track system performance and automatically scale resources up or down based on demand[3][4][5].

Case Studies and Examples

Case Study 1: Twitter's Microservices Architecture

Twitter, one of the most popular social media platforms, relies on a distributed architecture to handle its massive user base and high traffic. Their system consists of multiple microservices that work together to provide various functionalities. Each microservice is responsible for a specific task, such as handling tweets, user authentication, or recommendation algorithms. These microservices communicate with each other using lightweight protocols like HTTP or a message broker such as Apache Kafka.

Key Takeaways:

- **Microservices**: Breaking down the application into smaller services allows for independent development, deployment, and scaling.

- **Load Balancing**: Distributing requests across multiple servers ensures that no single server becomes a bottleneck.
- **Caching**: Using caching mechanisms to store frequently accessed data reduces the load on the database and improves response times[6].

Case Study 2: Netflix's Content Delivery Network (CDN)

Netflix, a leading streaming service, uses a highly scalable content delivery network to deliver video content to millions of users worldwide. Their CDN, called Open Connect, involves strategically placing servers close to users to reduce latency and improve streaming quality. Netflix also uses adaptive bitrate streaming to adjust the video quality based on the user's internet connection.

Key Takeaways:

- **CDN**: Using a content delivery network to distribute content closer to users reduces latency and improves performance.
- **Adaptive Streaming**: Adjusting video quality based on network conditions ensures a smooth viewing experience.
- **Monitoring and Analytics**: Continuously monitoring network performance and user behavior helps in optimizing the delivery of content[7].

Case Study 3: Amazon's DynamoDB

Amazon DynamoDB is a fully managed NoSQL database service designed for high availability and scalability. It uses a distributed architecture to automatically partition data across multiple servers. DynamoDB also provides features like automatic scaling, backup and restore, and in-memory caching.

Key Takeaways:

- **Distributed Architecture**: Partitioning data across multiple servers ensures high availability and fault tolerance.
- **Automatic Scaling**: Dynamically adjusting resources based on demand

helps in managing varying workloads.
- **NoSQL Database**: Using a NoSQL database allows for flexible data modeling and efficient handling of large datasets[8].

Summary

System design is a critical skill for building robust, scalable, and efficient systems. By understanding the basics of system design, applying principles for scalability, and learning from real-world case studies, you can develop systems that meet the needs of users and businesses. Whether you're designing a social media platform, a streaming service, or a database system, the principles of system design will guide you in creating solutions that are both effective and scalable.

Behavioral Questions

Common Behavioral Questions
Behavioral interview questions are designed to assess how you've handled various situations in the past, which can be indicative of how you'll perform in the future. These questions often start with phrases like "Tell me about a time when…" or "Give me an example of…". Here are some common categories of behavioral questions:

1. Teamwork:

- "Tell me about a time when you worked as part of a team."
- "Describe a situation where you had to collaborate with a difficult team member."

2. Problem-Solving:

- "Give me an example of a problem you faced at work and how you solved it."
- "Describe a challenging situation and how you handled it."

3. Leadership:

- "Tell me about a time when you led a project."
- "Describe a situation where you had to motivate others."

4. Adaptability:

- "Give me an example of a time when you had to adapt to a significant change."
- "Describe a situation where you had to learn something new quickly."

5. Conflict Resolution:

- "Tell me about a time when you had a conflict with a coworker and how you resolved it."
- "Describe a situation where you had to mediate a dispute."

6. Time Management:

- "Give me an example of how you manage your time when working on multiple projects."
- "Describe a situation where you had to meet a tight deadline."

7. Failure and Learning:

- "Tell me about a time when you failed and what you learned from it."
- "Describe a situation where you made a mistake and how you handled it."

These questions help interviewers understand your soft skills, such as communication, teamwork, and problem-solving abilities[12].

STAR Method for Answering

The STAR method is a structured approach to answering behavioral interview questions. STAR stands for Situation, Task, Action, and Result. This method helps you create clear, concise, and compelling responses by breaking down your answer into four parts:

1. **Situation**: Describe the context within which you performed a task or faced a challenge. Be specific about the situation to provide a clear background.
2. **Task**: Explain the actual task or challenge that was involved. What was

your responsibility or goal in that situation?
3. **Action**: Describe the specific actions you took to address the task or challenge. Focus on what you did, how you did it, and why you chose those actions.
4. **Result**: Share the outcomes or results of your actions. What was the impact of your efforts? If possible, quantify the results to provide a clear picture of your success.

Example: "Tell me about a time when you had to manage a difficult project."

Situation: "In my previous role as a project manager, we had a project with a tight deadline and limited resources."

Task: "My task was to ensure the project was completed on time without compromising quality."

Action: "I organized a series of planning meetings to break down the project into manageable tasks. I delegated responsibilities based on team members' strengths and set up a tracking system to monitor progress. I also communicated regularly with stakeholders to manage expectations and address any issues promptly."

Result: "As a result, we completed the project two days ahead of schedule and received positive feedback from the client for our efficiency and quality of work. This led to a 20% increase in repeat business from that client."

Using the STAR method helps you provide structured and detailed answers that highlight your skills and achievements[34].

Examples and Practice

Practicing your responses to behavioral questions using the STAR method can help you feel more confident and prepared for your interview. Here are some examples and practice questions to get you started:

Example 1: Teamwork

Question: "Tell me about a time when you worked as part of a team to achieve a goal."

Situation: "In my role as a marketing coordinator, our team was tasked with launching a new product."

Task: "My responsibility was to coordinate the social media campaign."

Action: "I collaborated with the design team to create engaging content, scheduled posts to align with our overall marketing strategy, and monitored engagement to adjust our approach as needed."

Result: "The campaign resulted in a 30% increase in social media followers and a 15% increase in product sales within the first month."

Example 2: Problem-Solving

Question: "Give me an example of a problem you faced at work and how you solved it."

Situation: "As a customer service representative, I encountered a situation where a customer was unhappy with a product they received."

Task: "My task was to resolve the customer's issue and ensure their satisfaction."

Action: "I listened to the customer's concerns, apologized for the inconvenience, and offered a replacement product. I also provided a discount on their next purchase as a goodwill gesture."

Result: "The customer was satisfied with the resolution and left a positive review, which helped improve our overall customer satisfaction rating."

Practice Questions:

1. **Leadership**: "Describe a situation where you had to lead a team through a challenging project."
2. **Adaptability**: "Tell me about a time when you had to adapt to a significant change at work."
3. **Conflict Resolution**: "Give me an example of a conflict you had with a coworker and how you resolved it."
4. **Time Management**: "Describe a situation where you had to manage multiple priorities and meet tight deadlines."
5. **Failure and Learning**: "Tell me about a time when you failed at a task and what you learned from the experience."

When practicing, try to use the STAR method to structure your responses. This will help you provide clear and detailed answers that demonstrate your skills and experiences effectively[125].

Summary

Behavioral questions are a crucial part of the interview process, allowing employers to gauge your past behavior and predict your future performance. By understanding common behavioral questions and using the STAR method to structure your answers, you can provide compelling and detailed responses that highlight your skills and experiences. Practicing these responses will help you feel more confident and prepared for your next interview.

Mock Interviews

Conducting Mock Interviews

Mock interviews are practice sessions that simulate real job interviews. They help candidates prepare for actual interviews by providing a realistic environment to practice responses, improve communication skills, and receive feedback. Here's how to conduct effective mock interviews:

1. **Choose the Right Interviewer**: Select someone who can provide constructive feedback. This could be a career counselor, mentor, colleague, or even a friend with experience in interviewing. Ideally, the interviewer should have knowledge of the industry or role you are targeting[12].
2. **Set Up a Realistic Environment**: Mimic the actual interview setting as closely as possible. If the real interview is virtual, conduct the mock interview online using the same platform. If it's in-person, choose a quiet, professional setting. Dress appropriately to get into the right mindset[34].
3. **Prepare Questions**: Compile a list of common interview questions relevant to the job. Include a mix of behavioral, technical, and situational questions. This helps in covering various aspects of the interview process[12].
4. **Conduct the Interview**: Start with a brief introduction and proceed with the questions. The interviewer should take notes on the candidate's responses, body language, and overall demeanor. Encourage the

candidate to answer questions as they would in a real interview[56].

5. **Provide Feedback**: After the interview, discuss the candidate's performance. Highlight strengths and areas for improvement. Be specific with your feedback, providing examples and suggestions for better responses[12].

6. **Record the Session**: If possible, record the mock interview. This allows the candidate to review their performance and identify areas for improvement. Watching the recording can provide insights into non-verbal communication and overall presentation[37].

7. **Repeat the Process**: Conduct multiple mock interviews to help the candidate refine their skills. Each session should focus on different aspects of the interview process, such as answering difficult questions, improving body language, or managing stress[58].

Analyzing Performance

Analyzing performance in mock interviews is crucial for identifying strengths and areas for improvement. Here's how to effectively analyze performance:

1. **Review Responses**: Evaluate the candidate's answers to each question. Check for clarity, relevance, and completeness. Were the responses structured and to the point? Did the candidate use the STAR method (Situation, Task, Action, Result) for behavioral questions[9,10]?

2. **Assess Communication Skills**: Pay attention to both verbal and non-verbal communication. Verbal communication includes tone, pitch, and clarity of speech. Non-verbal communication includes body language, eye contact, and facial expressions. Effective communication is key to making a positive impression[11,12].

3. **Evaluate Confidence and Poise**: Confidence is a critical factor in interviews. Assess how confidently the candidate presented themselves. Did they maintain eye contact? Were they able to handle difficult questions without getting flustered[10,13]?

4. **Check for Preparation**: Determine if the candidate was well-prepared.

Did they research the company and role? Were they able to articulate why they are a good fit for the position? Preparation shows dedication and interest in the job[9][10].
5. **Identify Strengths and Weaknesses**: Highlight the candidate's strengths, such as strong communication skills, relevant experience, or a positive attitude. Also, identify areas for improvement, such as better structuring of answers, reducing filler words, or improving body language[13][14].
6. **Provide Constructive Feedback**: Offer specific, actionable feedback. Instead of saying "You need to improve your answers," provide examples like "Try to structure your answers using the STAR method for better clarity." Constructive feedback helps candidates understand exactly what they need to work on[10][13].
7. **Use Performance Metrics**: If possible, use performance metrics to quantify the candidate's performance. This could include scoring their responses on a scale of 1 to 5, rating their communication skills, or assessing their overall confidence. Metrics provide a clear, objective way to measure improvement over time[9][10].
8. **Follow-Up**: After providing feedback, schedule follow-up sessions to track the candidate's progress. Continuous improvement is key to mastering interview skills[10][13].

Improving Interview Skills

Improving interview skills is an ongoing process that involves practice, feedback, and self-reflection. Here are some strategies to enhance your interview skills:

1. **Practice Regularly**: Regular practice is essential for improving interview skills. Conduct mock interviews frequently to build confidence and refine your responses. Practice helps in becoming more comfortable with the interview format and questions[11][12].
2. **Use the STAR Method**: The STAR method (Situation, Task, Action, Result) is a powerful tool for answering behavioral questions. It helps

in structuring responses clearly and concisely. Practice using the STAR method to ensure your answers are well-organized and impactful[11][12].

3. **Research the Company**: Thoroughly research the company and the role you are applying for. Understand the company's mission, values, products, and recent news. This knowledge helps in tailoring your responses to align with the company's goals and culture[11][12].

4. **Prepare Your Elevator Pitch**: An elevator pitch is a brief summary of who you are, what you do, and what you are looking for. It's a great way to introduce yourself at the beginning of an interview. Practice your elevator pitch to ensure it's concise and compelling[11][12].

5. **Improve Non-Verbal Communication**: Non-verbal communication plays a significant role in interviews. Practice maintaining good eye contact, using appropriate gestures, and having a confident posture. Non-verbal cues can enhance your verbal responses and make a positive impression[11][12].

6. **Manage Stress and Anxiety**: Interviews can be stressful, but managing stress is crucial for performing well. Practice relaxation techniques such as deep breathing, visualization, or mindfulness to stay calm and focused during the interview[11][12].

7. **Seek Feedback**: After each mock interview, seek feedback from your interviewer. Constructive feedback helps in identifying areas for improvement and provides guidance on how to enhance your performance. Be open to feedback and use it to make necessary adjustments[11][12].

8. **Record and Review**: Recording your mock interviews allows you to review your performance objectively. Watch the recordings to identify any habits or behaviors that need improvement. Self-review helps in becoming more aware of your strengths and weaknesses[11][12].

9. **Prepare Questions for the Interviewer**: Having thoughtful questions for the interviewer shows your interest in the role and company. Prepare a list of questions about the company's culture, team structure, or growth opportunities. Asking questions also helps in making the interview more interactive[11][12].

10. **Reflect and Refine**: After each interview, take time to reflect on your performance. Identify what went well and what could be improved. Use this reflection to refine your approach for future interviews. <u>Continuous self-improvement is key to mastering interview skills</u>[11][12].

Summary

Mock interviews are an invaluable tool for preparing for real job interviews. By conducting realistic practice sessions, analyzing performance, and continuously improving interview skills, candidates can enhance their confidence and effectiveness in interviews. Regular practice, constructive feedback, and self-reflection are essential components of this process. Whether you are a job seeker or someone helping others prepare for interviews, understanding and applying these principles can lead to successful interview outcomes.

Appendices

Python Standard Library

The **Python Standard Library** is a collection of modules and packages that come bundled with Python. It provides a wide range of functionalities, from basic data types and file I/O to more complex operations like web development and data analysis. Here are some key components:

1. **Built-in Functions**: Python includes numerous built-in functions like print(), len(), and range(), which are always available without needing to import any module.
2. **Data Types**: The library includes modules for various data types:

- **collections**: Provides specialized container datatypes like namedtuples, deque, Counter, and OrderedDict.
- **array**: Offers efficient arrays of numeric values.
- **datetime**: Supplies classes for manipulating dates and times.

3. **File and Directory Access**:

- **os**: Provides a way of using operating system-dependent functionality like reading or writing to the file system.
- **shutil**: Offers high-level operations on files and collections of files, such

as copying and archiving.

4. Data Persistence:

- **pickle**: Allows for serializing and deserializing Python object structures.
- **sqlite3**: Provides a lightweight disk-based database that doesn't require a separate server process.

5. Internet Data Handling:

- **urllib**: Handles fetching data across the web.
- **http**: Contains modules for handling HTTP requests and responses.

6. Text Processing:

- **re**: Supports regular expressions for advanced string processing.
- **string**: Contains common string operations and constants.

7. Mathematical Operations:

- **math**: Provides access to mathematical functions like trigonometry, logarithms, and factorials.
- **random**: Implements pseudo-random number generators for various distributions.

The Python Standard Library is extensive and designed to provide a solid foundation for most programming tasks[1][2][3].

Common Algorithms and Data Structures

Understanding **algorithms and data structures** is crucial for solving complex problems efficiently. Here are some of the most common ones:

1. Data Structures:

- **Arrays**: Fixed-size data structures that store elements of the same type.

- **Linked Lists**: Collections of nodes where each node contains data and a reference to the next node.
- **Stacks**: LIFO (Last In, First Out) data structures used for tasks like expression evaluation and backtracking.
- **Queues**: FIFO (First In, First Out) data structures used in scenarios like task scheduling.
- **Trees**: Hierarchical data structures with nodes connected by edges. Binary trees, AVL trees, and red-black trees are common types.
- **Graphs**: Collections of nodes (vertices) connected by edges. Used to represent networks.
- **Hash Tables**: Data structures that map keys to values for efficient data retrieval.

2. **Algorithms**:

- **Sorting Algorithms**: Methods to arrange data in a particular order. Examples include Quick Sort, Merge Sort, and Bubble Sort.
- **Searching Algorithms**: Techniques to find specific elements within data structures. Examples include Binary Search and Linear Search.
- **Graph Algorithms**: Algorithms to traverse or find paths in graphs. Examples include Depth-First Search (DFS), Breadth-First Search (BFS), and Dijkstra's Algorithm.
- **Dynamic Programming**: A method for solving complex problems by breaking them down into simpler subproblems. Examples include the Fibonacci sequence and the 0/1 Knapsack Problem.
- **Greedy Algorithms**: Algorithms that make the locally optimal choice at each step. Examples include the Fractional Knapsack Problem and Prim's Algorithm for Minimum Spanning Trees[4][5][6].

Interview Preparation Checklist

Preparing for an interview involves several steps to ensure you present yourself effectively. Here's a comprehensive checklist:

1. **Research the Company**: Understand the company's mission, values, products, and recent news. This helps tailor your responses to align with the company's goals.
2. **Review the Job Description**: Analyze the job requirements and responsibilities to understand what the employer is looking for.
3. **Prepare Your Resume**: Ensure your resume is up-to-date and tailored to the job you're applying for. Highlight relevant experiences and skills.
4. **Practice Common Interview Questions**: Prepare answers for common questions like:

- "Tell me about yourself."
- "Why do you want to work here?"
- "What are your strengths and weaknesses?"

5. **Use the STAR Method**: Structure your answers to behavioral questions using the Situation, Task, Action, Result (STAR) method.

6. **Prepare Questions for the Interviewer**: Have thoughtful questions ready to ask the interviewer about the company, team, and role.

7. **Dress Appropriately**: Choose professional attire that fits the company's culture.

8. **Plan Your Journey**: Ensure you know the interview location and plan your route to arrive on time.

9. **Bring Necessary Documents**: Carry multiple copies of your resume, a list of references, and any other required documents.

10. **Follow Up**: Send a thank-you email after the interview to express your appreciation and reiterate your interest in the position[789].

Additional Resources

To further enhance your knowledge and skills, consider exploring these additional resources:

1. **Online Courses and Tutorials**:

- **Coursera**: Offers courses on various topics, including programming, data science, and machine learning.

- **edX**: Provides courses from top universities on a wide range of subjects.
- **Khan Academy**: Offers free tutorials on computer science and programming.

2. **Books**:

- **"Cracking the Coding Interview" by Gayle Laakmann McDowell**: A comprehensive guide to technical interviews.
- **"Introduction to Algorithms" by Thomas H. Cormen, Charles E. Leiserson, Ronald L. Rivest, and Clifford Stein**: A detailed book on algorithms and data structures.
- **"Design Patterns: Elements of Reusable Object-Oriented Software" by Erich Gamma, Richard Helm, Ralph Johnson, and John Vlissides**: A classic book on software design patterns.

3. **Coding Practice Platforms**:

- **LeetCode**: Provides a vast collection of coding problems and contests.
- **HackerRank**: Offers coding challenges and competitions to improve your skills.
- **CodeSignal**: Provides coding assessments and interview practice.

4. **Community and Forums**:

- **Stack Overflow**: A community of programmers where you can ask questions and share knowledge.
- **Reddit**: Subreddits like r/learnprogramming and r/cscareerquestions offer advice and resources for programmers.

5. **Documentation and References**:

- **Python Documentation**: The official documentation for Python, including the standard library and tutorials.

- **GeeksforGeeks**: A website with tutorials and articles on various programming topics.
- **W3Schools**: Provides tutorials on web development technologies[10][11][12].

Summary

The appendices provide valuable information and resources to support your learning and preparation for programming interviews. The Python Standard Library offers a wide range of functionalities, while common algorithms and data structures form the foundation of problem-solving skills. An interview preparation checklist ensures you are well-prepared for interviews, and additional resources help you continue learning and improving your skills. By leveraging these tools and strategies, you can enhance your knowledge and increase your chances of success in programming interviews.

www.ingramcontent.com/pod-product-compliance
Lightning Source LLC
Chambersburg PA
CBHW070425240526
45472CB00020B/1325